Traditions Around The World

Games

by Godfrey Hall

Thomson Learning
New York

Traditions Around The World

Body Decoration

Costumes

Dance

Food

Games

Jewelry

Masks

Musical Instruments

COVER: Buddhist monks playing Chess in a Bangkok monastery, Thailand.

Consultant: Anthony Shelton, Keeper of Non-Western Art and Anthropology, Royal Pavilion Art Gallery and Museums, Brighton, East Sussex, England.

First published in the
United States in 1995 by
Thomson Learning
115 Fifth Avenue
New York, NY 10003

First published in Great Britain in 1995 by
Wayland (Publishers) Ltd.

U.K. version copyright © 1995 Wayland (Publishers) Ltd.

U.S. version copyright © 1995 Thomson Learning

Library of Congress Cataloging-in-Publication Data
Hall, Godfrey.
  Games / by Godfrey Hall.
    p.   cm.—(Traditions around the world)
  "First published in Great Britain in 1995 by Wayland (Publishers) Ltd."—T.p. verso.
  Includes bibliographical references and index.
  ISBN 1-56847-345-1
  1. Games—Juvenile literature. 2. Manners and customs—Juvenile literature. [1. Games. 2. Manners and customs.]
I. Title. II. Series.
GV1201.H32   1995
790.1—dc20   94-39447

Printed in Italy

Acknowledgments:

The publishers wish to thank the following for providing the photographs for this book: Brian and Cherry Alexander 16-17 (all), 26, 36; J. Allan Cash Ltd. 8, 9, 31 (left); Sue Cunningham Photographic 23, 24; Ebenezer Pictures 25; Eye Ubiquitous *cover*, 10 (David Cumming), 20 (E. J. B. Hawkins), 28-29 (both, left L. Foroyee, right John Hulme), 30 (top, P.M. Field), 31 (right), 32 (bottom, Julia Waterlow); Jim Holmes 32 (top); Hutchison Library 6-7, 35 (Nancy Durrell McKenna), 37 (bottom, Liz McLeod), 41 (Michael Macintyre); Life File 37 (top, Andy Teare); Nintendo 19; Christine Osborne 33, 42-43; Tony Stone Worldwide, 6 (Julian Engelsman), 13, 18, 43 (David Hiser); Wayland Picture Library 11, 12 (both), 15.

Artwork by Pauline Allen. Maps by Peter Bull.

The author would like to thank the following for their kind help and cooperation in the writing of this book:
Reinhard Batz and Marion and Wolfram Gebauer, Germany; Joan and Harold Vidler, Australia; Susannah Langton, SFB Ltd.; Singapore National Library; Ari Saari, Finland; Dr. Ibtissam Al-Bassam; King Fahad Academy, London; Jenny Tegnhed, Swedish Travel and Tourism Council, London; Karim Ebrahim Al-Shaktar, U.K. Ambassador for Bahrain; Mike Theobald; Evelyn Lafone, Swiss National Tourist Office; Maria Thorn.

Contents

Games around the world

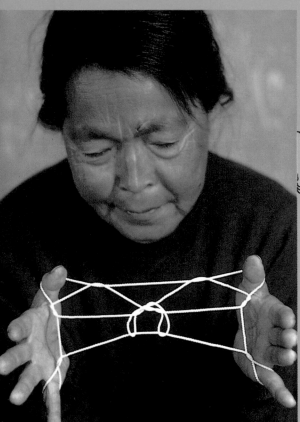

▲ String puzzles are important traditional games among Native Americans. The patterns are often used to tell stories.

▲ Men playing a ball game in Barcelona, Spain.

4

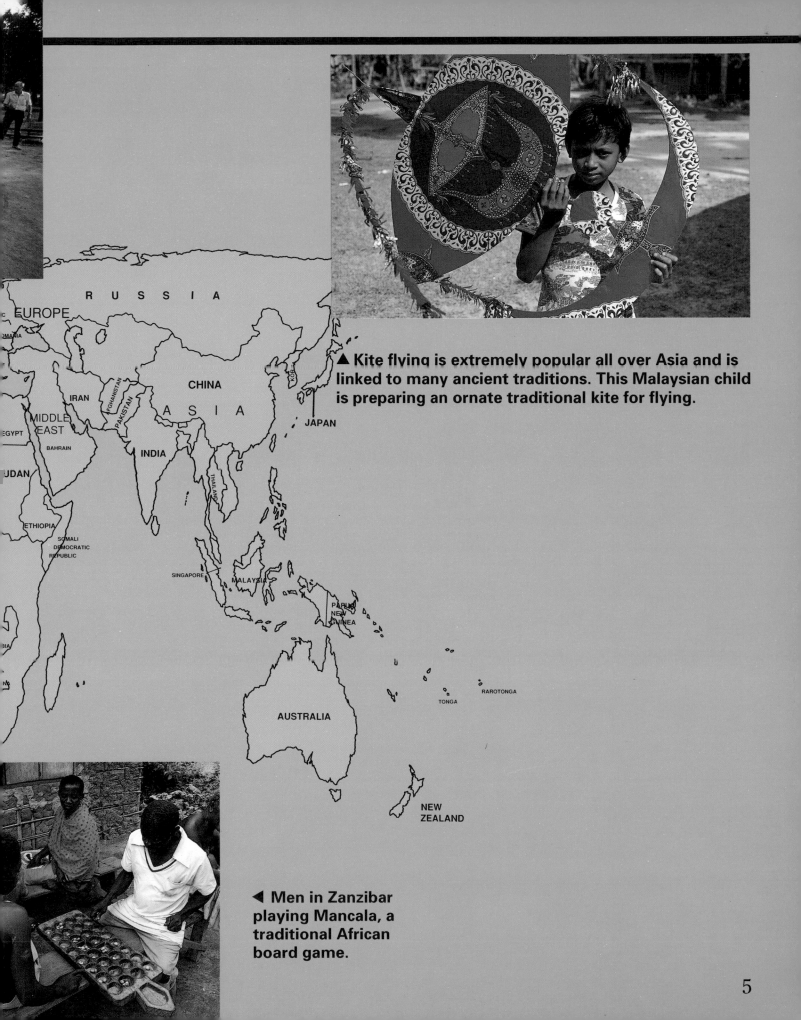

▲ Kite flying is extremely popular all over Asia and is linked to many ancient traditions. This Malaysian child is preparing an ornate traditional kite for flying.

◀ Men in Zanzibar playing Mancala, a traditional African board game.

Introduction

Cultures all over the world have traditional games that have been played for centuries and passed from generation to generation by word of mouth. And new games are continually being invented and developed that reflect the cultures of today.

The need for people to find ways to amuse themselves and have fun has led to an enormous variety of games. Yet games played in remote corners of the world can be very similar to those found in large developed cities. Go anywhere in the world and children may be seen playing Hide-and-Seek, Marbles, or Leap Frog. Rules do vary, however, from region to region. Other games, such as Hurling in Ireland or Pesa Pallo in Finland are not played much beyond the countries where they originated.

Games can be played by one person, such as the card game Solitaire, or they may involve groups of players sometimes divided into teams. People enjoy playing games indoors, what were once known as "parlor games." Along with card games, people enjoy

People playing cards in ▶
Shanghai. Card games are
very popular in China, and
all around the world.

6

▲ **Marbles is played on streets and in playgrounds world-wide. These children in Calcutta, India, are playing their own version of the game.**

board games and computer games. Word games like Hangman are also enjoyed.

For outdoor recreation, people enjoy physical challenges. Games are played on city streets, stoops, and in parks and fields throughout the world. Though sports involve organized formal athletic activities, they too are a type of game because basketball and football players share what is common to all games players—the desire to win.

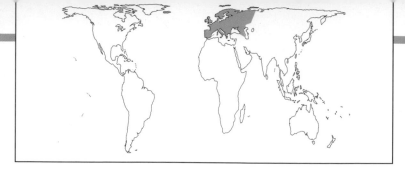

Europe

Many of the games played in Europe can be found elsewhere in the world and may have been introduced by Europeans when they traveled from place to place.

Examples of this include British Bulldog, a game where players have to cross a space without being caught. Emigrants from Victorian England probably took this game to Australia, where it is known as Australian Dingo. It is also similar to a game played in the United States called Tom Tiddler's Ground, in which children have to run across a forbidden area and are taken prisoner if caught. This game may have been brought to the United States by early European settlers in the colonial era.

Some games have been popular for centuries, such as Hide-and-Seek. This is played by children everywhere and has been given a variety of names. Some of its rules are said to date back thousands of years: it was known as Apodidraskinda in ancient Greece. It is mentioned in Shakespeare—the cry "All Hid" meant the start of the game—and was known as Hospy in nineteenth-century Scotland. In one early version the word "Whoop" meant it was time for the searcher to go off and find the others.

What's the Time, Mr. Wolf? is played by children all over Europe throughout the year. One child is Mr. Wolf and the others follow him or her. As they follow they call out, "What's the time, Mr. Wolf?" The wolf calls out different times, but suddenly shouts "Dinner time!," turns around and chases the others back to the starting line. If anyone is caught, that player becomes Mr Wolf.

The ancient Romans played various dice games. The board for this one has been scratched into the stone at the forum in Rome, Italy. ▼

Games such as Hook the ▶ Fish are played at English fairs during the summer.

Certain games in Europe are similar but may be called different names and played with different rules. Wie Tief ist das Wasser? (How Deep is the Water?) from Germany is known in England as Farmer, Farmer, May We Cross Your River?, while outside Europe in Zambia there is a similar game called Crocodile, May I Cross the River?

one of them. In Germany this game is known as Nix in der Grube (Water Nymphs in the Pit). In this version, the person in the middle is a water sprite. In Greece it is called The Tortoise and in the Czech Republic it is known as Prinzessin Erlösen (Sleeping Princess). Here the players walk around the figure in the center, "Death," counting the hours on the clock. Each time they count out the chimes, Death tells them that they must sleep. At midnight, Death springs to life and tries to catch them.

Blind Man's Buff is a very old game that is popular around the world. It dates back to the fourteenth century, and was probably played at early fairs and festivals in Europe. One of the first versions was known as Hood Man Blind. To play the game, one person is blindfolded and put into the center of a circle of people. He or she is turned around several times. The player then has to catch someone and figure out who it is. In Austria the game is called Blinde Kuh (Blind Cow), and the person who is caught becomes the cow. In Sweden it is known as Blind Bock, and a game called Blind Cat is played in Greece and Spain.

Some European games are only played in one particular area or country. These may be linked with local events or religious festivals.

Dead Man Arise, another popular game, probably started when children began to act out an ancient horror story about a "green lady," who refused to leave her room. In the end, after calling several times, her servant went upstairs to fetch her. Looking through the keyhole, she saw the lady dancing in a bowl of blood.

In Dead Man Arise, one person lies on the ground covered in a coat or blanket. The other children walk around him or her, calling out "Dead man, arise." When they least expect it, the person under the coat leaps up and tries to catch

There are a large number of local festivals held all over Switzerland every year. Part of the winter festival in Halwill includes a November whip-cracking competition. In early December, six of the winning whip crackers travel around the village dressed as mischievous spirits, visiting homes and giving out presents to the children or warnings if they are naughty.

Boules is one of the most popular games in France, especially in the south of the country. It is usually played during the summer in village squares. Two teams of three or four play, although they can sometimes be much larger.

A small ball, or cochonnet, is thrown onto a section of ground. Two teams then try to throw larger balls as close as possible to the cochonnet. The winner is the person who gets the ball closest to the cochonnet. That player then has the chance to throw the cochonnet and have the first turn to throw the larger balls. A team wins if its ball rolls nearest to the cochonnet the most times. There is no limit to the number of games that can be played.

▲ The French game of Boules is often played in village squares in the south of the country.

Hurling has been played for hundreds of years throughout Ireland. During the eighteenth century, large bets often were made on who might win. In 1769 a match was played for a bet of a dinner and a dance!

Hurling is very similar to hockey, but is played with a curved stick known as a hurley, that is wider and flatter than a hockey stick. The ball is known as a sliothar (or slitter) and is made of leather stuffed with animal hair. It can travel at speeds of up to 80 mph. There are fifteen players in each team, and the team that scores the most goals is the winner.

▲ Hurling is fast and furious and demands a great deal of skill.

▲ Curling, also known as Bowls on Ice, is a popular winter game in Scotland. It is played on ice, or on special cement "ponds."

Twisti is a very popular children's game in Finland, and versions of it are played all around the world. Twisti is played mainly by girls. Using a huge rubber band. One player stands inside the band at each end, while a third player jumps in and out with various moves and steps. The higher the band is moved, the more difficult the game. The game is similar to jump rope.

Pesa Pallo is an adult game played in Finland and Sweden. Played by men and women, it is similar to baseball and has nine players on each team. The game has nine innings, and the team that is batting tries to make as many runs as it can. The game was developed from the old ball games of Europe. It usually takes about two hours to play.

In Sweden, many people play a game called Hitta Nycklen (Hide the Key). One person hides something small in a room. The other players come into the room and ask questions that help them find the object. They can ask if a bird or fish could take it. If the answer is a bird, then the object is somewhere high, but if it is a fish it is hidden somewhere low.

Norway has a long coastline, and so the sea is an important part of its games tradition. A game played by Norwegian children is Bølge (Waves). Two lines are marked on the ground, one yard apart. One team is the waves. Small stones or shells are put in the space between the lines to represent the beach. The waves team stands behind one of the lines, holding hands and swinging backward and forward, saying "one, two, three, swish." While this is going on, a second team has to pick up the stones or shells from the beach. When the waves call out "swish," the others have to run back over the other line before the waves catch them. Anyone who is caught becomes a wave. This goes on until there is no one left to catch.

Play the game: How Deep Is the Water?

This popular game is from Germany, though a number of different versions are played elsewhere in Europe, and may have traveled with soldiers as they moved from country to country during wartime.

1. Draw two lines on the ground, 15 feet apart. These are the banks, and the space between them is the river.

2. One player stands on one bank and is called the fisherman. All the others stand on the other bank, facing the fisherman.

3. The other players call out: "How deep is the water?" The fisherman answers with any figure, 15 feet for example. The others reply: "How can we come over?"

4. The fisherman now tells the other players how they must cross the river, such as swimming. They then have to "swim" across the river. The fisherman has to tag them before they can cross the river.

5. The people who are tagged join the fisherman and help catch the next group. The last player remaining then becomes the fisherman.

Catching and chasing games ▶ are popular with children all over Europe and all around the world. Many games have similar origins and aims, but are played slightly differently in different places.

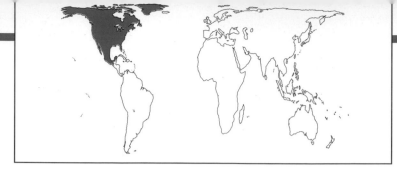

North America

In North America, there are many games of European origin, which were brought over by early settlers and immigrants. These include Charley Over the Water, or Baste the Bear, where a catcher has to sit in the middle of a circle while the others dance round him or her. Catching games are very popular in America and include a game called Molly Bright, which is played in parts of North Carolina. In this game there are two groups on either side and a person representing a witch in the middle. The game begins by one person calling out from one side to the other, "How many miles to Molly Bright?" The others call out, "Three score and ten." The other player calls out, "Can I get there by candlelight?" The reply is, "Yes, if your legs are long and light, but watch out for the old witch on the way." Both groups then run across the gap and try to get to the other side before the witch catches them. Another name for this game is How Many Miles to Babylon.

▲ These Inuit boys are playing Pull the Lazy Stick, a traditional game that is popular all over North America and similar to Tug-of-War. The aim of the game is to pull your opponent into your own area.

Apache boys climbing ▶ a slippery pole in New Mexico. This game symbolizes the fact that they have reached puberty.

Although there are many games in North America that have their roots in Europe, some are much older, such as those played by Native American and Inuit peoples. Originally, their games were linked with traditional myths or gods or were played at ceremonies and festivals. These include many ball games and team games, such as Canadian Snowshoeing. This was started in the nineteenth century by the *coureurs du bois* (runners of the wood), the animal trappers who wore light snowshoes to get to their traps quickly. Snowshoeing is still played today.

Inuit children in northern Canada and Alaska play Muk (Silence). One player goes into the center of a circle of players and picks out one other person, who must then stay silent and serious. The player in the center tries to make him or her laugh by making faces. If the other person laughs, he or she must go into the center.

Computer games, which ▶ were invented in North America, have become very popular in many countries.

◀ Lacrosse is played by teams of ten men or twelve women. The players use special sticks with nets designed to catch the ball and throw it powerfully.

Another popular game is Lacrosse, which is now an international sport. This tough game was originally used by the Huron indians to train their warriors and was called Bagataway. Two teams of ten men or twelve women, using long sticks with a net at one end, try to throw a ball into the other team's goal. Many years ago Huron teams could have up to one hundred players on each side. Fast-moving team games are an important Native American tradition. Originally, they were played to develop strength and speed, and as competitions between rival villages.

Bilboquet, a traditional Inuit game, uses a wooden ball full of holes that must be caught on a wooden spike. Originally, the ball was carved from a piece of bone into the shape of a bear's head, and competitions were held every year. The game sometimes accompanied a story. Each hole in the ball represented an event in the story, and the holes had to be speared in the right order.

Recently, computer games have become a very popular pastime in Canada and the United States, as well as in many other countries. They are usually played by one person at home.

One of the first computer games to appear was Pong, developed by Nolan Bushnell in 1972. Two players hit a ball from one side of the screen to the other. Pac-man and Space Invaders quickly followed this. Pac-man featured a creature that ate things, and Space Invaders involved firing at an endless number of attacking spaceships.

Many of the ideas used in electronic games have been around a long time and are connected with chasing, hiding, and fighting. These are ideas that have been used in traditional children's games for centuries.

The Maya people were living in Mexico and Central America as long ago as 1500 B.C. They built magnificent cities and roads, many of which still survive. They had special ball courts in which they played a game called Tlatchi.

One of the greatest Mayan cities was at Chichén Itzá in the Yucatán, Mexico. The city contained ornate temples and huge halls, and its ball court was about three hundred feet long and one hundred feet wide. This is where Tlatchi was played. Two teams each tried to get a heavy rubber ball through a stone ring. The game was very difficult and fast. It is said that the losing team had their heads chopped off and displayed as a sacrifice to the gods, although we do not know if this is true. Tlatchi was played by peoples all over Mexico and Central America, and was known by many different names, such as Hulama and Tzalatz.

The great Mayan civilization came to an end about 1,100 years ago, when the cities were abandoned. It is now believed that the civilization collapsed due to over-farming of the environment and a great increase in warfare against other peoples. Today, many descendants of the Maya live in the Yucatán Peninsula and Guatemala, and speak Mayan as well as Spanish.

The ruins of a Mayan ball ▶ court in the Yucatán, Mexico. The players had to throw a heavy rubber ball through this stone ring.

Play the game: Jacks

Jacks has been played all over the world for many centuries. It was popular among many Native Americans, and originally was probably played with bones as jacks.

You will need:
a small rubber ball
6–12 six-pointed jacks (if you do not have jacks, use seeds, twigs, or small stones)

1. Throw the jacks onto the playing surface.

2. Using the same hand, throw the ball up into the air and pick up one jack after the ball has bounced. Catch the ball with the same hand.

3. Next pick up two at a time, then three, and on up until six. The first player to complete all six steps without missing any jacks is the winner.

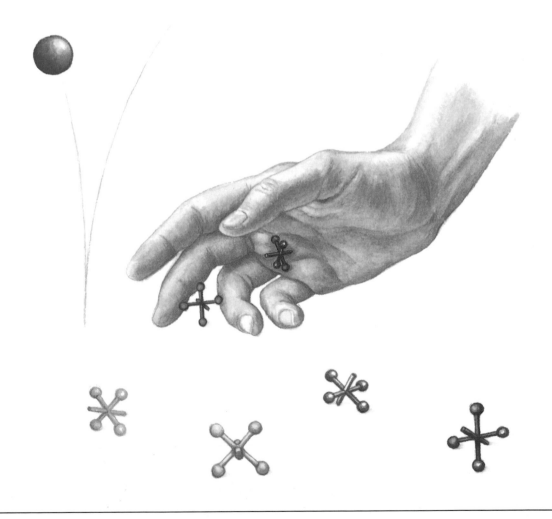

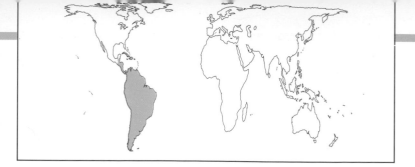

Central and South America

The original peoples of Central and South America played a wide variety of games. Most of the games now played in Central and South America had their roots in the Inca, Mayan, and Aztec civilizations, although some games may have arrived with the Spanish settlers who landed in South America in the sixteenth century.

Ball games are played by indigenous peoples all over Central and South America. Often balls made of corn leaves, rubber, or stuffed animal skin are used. These include team games between groups or villages in which the ball must be kept in the air using any part of the body except the hands and feet. Similar games are played using shuttlecocks of corn leaves in the Amazon and Orinoco regions, while in eastern Brazil and central South America the ball is volleyed with the hand or thrown.

Relay races are popular traditional team games. In eastern Brazil, they are played by men carrying sections of tree trunks that can weigh up to 200 pounds. Female players use lighter logs. Dice games are common among the peoples of the Andes region, where they use dice made of bone or wood.

Board games are often played outdoors in Central and South America. ▶

In Argentina, children play a game of Spanish origin called El Gato y el Raton (Cat and Mouse). The players join hands in a circle. One person stands inside the circle as the mouse, and one stands outside as the cat. The cat asks, "What are you doing in my vineyard?" The mouse answers, "Eating grapes." The cat then asks for some. The mouse reaches through the circle and says, "Here they are." The cat replies, "Give me more." The mouse says, "No." The cat says, "I'll catch you," and the mouse replies, "If you can." The cat then chases the mouse. If the mouse goes under two joined hands, he or she can leave the circle. If both the cat and the mouse are outside the circle, the mouse can go back in but the cat cannot. They change over when the mouse has been caught. This circle game is also played in Russia, Romania, and the United States.

In Peru and Guiana, many children's games are played outdoors. These include Hide-and-Seek, which is often played among the lime and guava trees, and which originated among the early peoples of the area. Children also play Jaguar, invented by the Makushí people. One child pretends to be a jaguar while the rest of the players line up in a row. The jaguar has to seize the last child in the line while the other players try to stop him or her. Further south, in Chile, groups of adults play a game called Rayuela. This uses heavy, bronze

◄ A favorite game of children in Brazil is Bumba-Meu-Boi. Here the players are putting on their costumes. The game involves a lot of dancing.

▲ Piñata is played all over Central and South America. These children in Guatemala are using a piñata shaped like a donkey.

discs called tejos, that are thrown toward a string stretched across one yard of damp ground. The object of the game is to throw the disks so they land on or near the string and push it down. The first person to hit the string a certain number of times is the winner. In cities such as Santiago there are special Rayuela grounds.

In Brazil, children play a game known as Hit It Off. They bang a piece of wood just over three feet high into the ground and draw two circles around it. One circle is drawn three feet from the pole and the other a foot away. They then put a coin on top of the stick. Each player has five pebbles. Standing by the outer circle, the players throw the pebbles and try to knock the coin off the pole. If the coin falls into the inner circle, the thrower scores one point. If it falls into the outer circle, two points are scored. The game goes on until the players decide to stop. The player who has scored the most points is the winner.

Play the game: Piñata

A traditional game played in Mexico during Christmastime, the piñata has become very popular for all festive occasions, especially birthdays. Piñatas can be made of papier-mâché, pottery, and even a cardboard box or paper bag. They are filled with candies and small surprises. Make sure you play this game somewhere in the open, for it can be very messy!

You will need:
a small cardboard box or paper bag
  filled with candy (the piñata)
a stick about three feet long
blindfolds
string or cord

1. Hang the piñata in an open area.

2. The first player puts on a blindfold and is turned around three times. He is then handed a stick and has three chances to hit the piñata to open it.

The game of Piñata ▶ has become popular all over the world. These children in Greenland, who live close to the Arctic Circle, are playing the game to welcome the sun at the beginning of the summer.

3. When a player hits the piñata so that it opens and the candies fall to the ground, all the players scurry to pick up the treats.

If a large group plays the game, more than one piñata may be used.

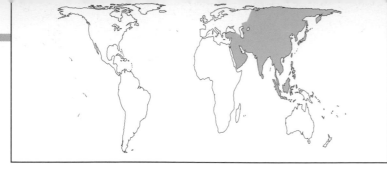

Asia

Many games in India have religious origins. Snakes and Ladders, a popular board game, started out as a Hindu game called Moksha-patamu. In this game, the snake represented evil and the ladder was a journey through life to heaven. Over the last one hundred years, Snakes and Ladders has changed into a simple race game. In China, a similar game called Shing Kun T'o is played.

A popular outdoor children's game in India is Lalamlai. This is played with short, thick sticks called dandas and a tennis ball. Each player moves into a space and draws a circle in the dirt around himself or herself. The ball is thrown as far away as possible. One player, who is "It," must pick it up and throw it back at the other players, trying to hit one of them or get the ball in one of their circles. If this happens, the player who has been hit becomes "It." The players in the circles can dodge the ball and hit it with their dandas. They must not use their hands.

A very popular game in Pakistan is Kokla-chaupakee. It can be played either in a small space such as a yard or out in the open. All the players except for one squat down in a circle facing the center. The remaining person runs around the outside of the circle with a piece of twisted material

Main picture: Monks playing Chess in a Bangkok monastery, Thailand.

In Bangladesh and other Asian ▶ countries, boys and girls will often play games separately.

and drops it behind one player. That person is allowed to feel for it but cannot turn around. If it is found, the person picks it up and chases the first person around the circle, trying to hit him or her with it before he or she gets back to the empty place. There are many other circle games played all over Asia.

Variations of one Afghan game, The Doorkeeper, are played all over the world. In Afghanistan, children play this in the street using a soft ball. The older the children, the smaller the ball. Players stand in a circle with their legs apart and their feet touching the next person's feet. One player stands in the center with the ball and tries to roll the ball through the legs of the others, who try to stop the ball by closing their legs. A player is out of the game if the ball goes between his or her legs. When everyone is out, the game starts again.

▲ **Mah Jongg is played all over China. It requires a lot of concentration.**

Backgammon, Mah Jongg, and card games are popular pastimes in the Far East, where they originated. They are now played all over the world.

Mah Jongg is a skillful game that is played a great deal in China. It is said to have been started by the boatmen living on the rivers. The cards they played with used to blow over the sides of the boats, so pieces of bamboo were stuck to the backs of the cards to stop this happening. Mah Jongg is usually played with 144 ivory, bamboo, or plastic tiles, divided into six suits (groups). The aim of the game is to obtain the most suits of tiles.

Backgammon is a board game for two players. It is played all over China and requires a lot of skill. It is played on a board split into two equal halves. Each player has fifteen stones or counters known as "men." The players throw two dice and move their pieces around the board. The first person to move all his or her pieces off the board is the winner.

In Korea, the Battle of the Wagons takes place at harvest time. Played by two teams called "East" and "West," this is a particularly noisy game. One member of each team, known as the cox, climbs to the top of the team's pole. The other players stay at the bottom, grip the poles, and move them according to orders shouted out by the cox. The winning team is the one that manages to knock the other team's cox off the pole. Originally, it was believed that if "West" won, the harvest would fail, and if "East" won, it would be successful.

In Thailand and other parts of Asia, games are often played using local materials. Takraw is played with a ball made out of hollow reeds. Any part of the body can be used to hit the ball, which must be kept off the ground at all times. There are many local variations of this game played throughout the country.

Spinning tops is popular all over the world, especially in Malaysia. This ancient activity was originally seen as a way of bringing in a good harvest. Gaming competitions would be held where people would see how long they could spin their tops. In the Kelantan area of Malaysia, there was a special ceremony in which the village leader's top was carried out of his house before the spinning started, accompanied by magic chants. The tops were usually spun inside a circle. The one whose top spun the longest was declared the winner.

In Singapore, many of the games played by children are linked with city life; today, electronic games are popular. Other games, such as Rubber Bands, probably arrived from other parts of the world due to Singapore's large immigrant population.

Rubber Bands is played mainly by boys. The bands are thrown, and if one touches another they are taken by the player who has thrown first. A popular game with boys living in the kampongs, or villages, is Main Lereng. This is played with the rim of a bicycle wheel, that is pushed with a long stick. Boys form teams and race against each other.

A traditional game played all over the Far East is Capte. This uses shuttlecocks made from a number of different animal skins, usually snake and shark skin, with three or more duck or chicken feathers. The shuttlecock, or capto, is kicked into the air using the right foot. Each player tries to keep it in the air until he or she misses, when the next player takes over. The first player to reach a certain number of kicks is the winner. When the game is played in teams, after a teammate misses the next team member continues. The first team to reach an agreed number of kicks is the winner.

◄ A Malaysian family playing a traditional game together.

▲ This top spinner in Malaysia is preparing to throw his top to make it spin.

31

In Asia, fruits and seeds are often used to form part of a game. Girls in Singapore play with the red heart-shaped seeds of the Arbus tree. The seeds are scattered on the floor, and each player traces an imaginary line from one seed to another. The players then flick one seed against the other. If the seeds touch, they take both seeds and have another two. Each player tries to collect as many seeds as possible.

One of the oldest games in the world is Go, which originated in China more than 4,000 years ago. It is also popular in Japan and is played on a board using about 150 black and white stones that represent day and night. There are over three hundred different ways of starting the game! Its object is to capture as much territory as possible with unbroken lines of stones. It is played by children and adults.

Jan-ken-pon is played by young Japanese children and is similar to the

Rock Paper Scissors game that is popular around the world. It is often played among children when they are trying to find a leader. A fist represents a rock; a hand represents paper; and two fingers mean scissors. Scissors cut paper; paper covers the rock; and the rock blunts the scissors. Each player decides which sign he or she is going to make, then all the players make their signs at the same time. Whoever has the most powerful sign wins the round. If two players make the same sign, the two must play again.

Children all over the world play Leap Frog. In Japan, this game is called Tobi Koshi. Children get into pairs and one bends over while the other runs up and vaults over his or her back. The jumper then bends over and the second player jumps over him or her. This continues until the pair has jumped all the way to the winning post.

▲ Go, one of the oldest games in the world, is played in China and Japan.

◀ **Japanese children playing Jan-ken-pon at a local festival. This game is played in many countries.**

Ear and Nose is a circle game played in Iran. The first person pulls the ear, hair, or nose of the person sitting on the left, who does the same. Once the action has gone around the circle, the first player then chooses a different part of the body to pull. Anyone who laughs is out of the game.

Many games need only simple equipment. A popular children's game in the Middle East requires nothing more than a piece of wood supported between two bricks and a stick. The top of the piece of wood is hit by the players with a stick about a foot long. As it is hit, it springs up. The winner is the one who can manage to make the stick go the highest.

Marbles is another popular game in the Middle East and elsewhere in the world, for it can be played anywhere and with any number of players.

Certain games are played in the Middle East during special occiasions. Ash-Zhalaalo, or Hit the Shadow, is played in the evening during Ramadan by both boys and girls in Bahrain. During Ramadan no one may eat during daylight. Everyone stands in a line, and one person leaves the line with a stick and asks, "What's your dinner tonight?" The answer from the line is "Mohammar" (sweet rice). The questioner then asks, "With what?" The reply is "Fried Saafi" (a local fish). The answer comes: "Why haven't you left me any?" They reply, "The cat has eaten it." The answer is "Take it then." The reply is "Let it come." The stick is then thrown onto the shadow of one of the players. This person picks up the stick and runs after the others. During the chase, he or she tries to step on the shadow of one of the other players. If this happens, that person takes over and becomes the questioner.

Kite flying is popular all ▶ over Asia. This ornate kite is being prepared for flying by a child in Malaysia.

Africa

Most African games, like many games around the world, are based on myths and legends, local animals and traditional ways of life. Many of the games are very old, such as the ancient Egyptian game Seega. This is similar to Tic-Tac-Toe. A crisscross pattern is drawn in the sand, and each player is given six stones. The aim of the game is to make a continuous line of stones. The players try to block each other's lines. Players can move their pieces one or two squares in any direction, but they cannot jump over another piece. The winner is the first to get three of his or her stones in a straight line. This is a simple modern version; traditional Seega is much more complicated.

Checkers is another game very popular in Egypt, where it has been played for hundreds of years. It is believed to have been invented in France in the twelfth century A.D. Played on a checkerboard, the object of the game is to capture or trap all of your opponent's pieces.

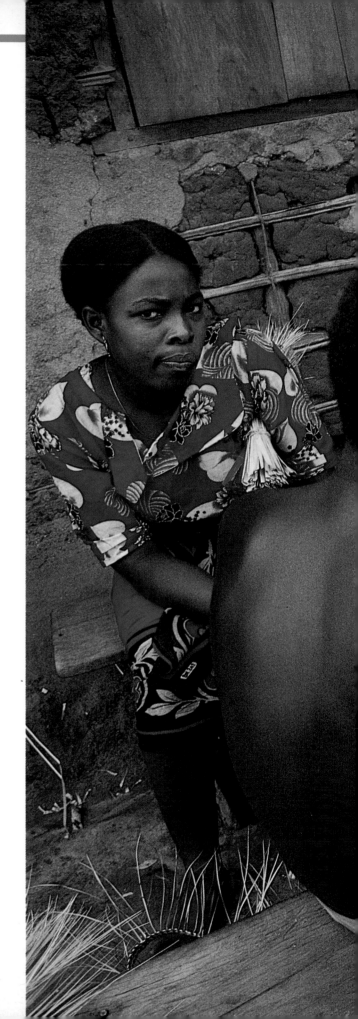

These men are playing ▶ a form of Mancala, an ancient traditional game that is played all over the African continent.

34

▲ **These Dogon boys in Mali have made their own bicycles out of natural materials.**

In the Sudan, children play a catching game called Leopard Trap. Two players make a trap with their arms outstretched and hands joined. The others form a long line and dance around, passing through the trap. As they do so they chant this rhyme:

"Lion and leopard
Lion and leopard
Two night hunters
Lion and leopard
Lion and leopard
Hunt their prey."

On the last word, the trap falls. If a player is caught, he or she is out of the game. Once two players have been caught, a second trap is made behind the first. The game continues until there are only two players left. They then make a new trap.

Hopscotch, which may have originated in Africa, has spread all over the world and is known by a number of names. In Germany it is called Hinkspiel and in India, Ekerid Dukaria. Libyan children play a version called Neggeza.

A pattern of squares is marked out in the sand and a stone is used as a marker. The first player hops on one foot, throwing the stone into square number 1, then 2, 3, 4 and so on. He or she must go on until the stone lands in the wrong square. That player then starts again when the others have had their turn. When a player completes the hopscotch, the player stands with his or her back to the pattern and throws the stone over his or her shoulder. If it lands in a square the player's initials are written in that square. This is now that player's square. No one else is allowed in it. The game continues until it is impossible to move without going into someone else's square. The player with the most squares wins.

Ayo is played all over Africa. It has been popular for thousands of years and has many different names: Wari, Awari, Bao, and Mankala, for example. The two-player game is based on harvest sowing traditions, and the aim is to sow as many beans, seeds, or shells as possible into fourteen holes dug in the ground or in a clay board until all the holes are filled. The rules of the game are very complicated, and skilled players play it at lightning speeds.

Cattle are an important part of African life, and a circle game from Botswana called Cattle Stockade is popular with children. The players hold hands in a circle and move around. Two players, or "cattle," stay in the center. They try to escape by running under the arms of the other players. The circle must not be broken. If they escape they join the circle, and two new players go into the center. Variations of this game are played elsewhere in the world, such as El Gato y el Raton in South America (see page 25)

In Benin, West Africa, young girls often play Dosu. A small object is hidden in a pile of sand. One pile is made for each player. Each person chooses a pile and tries to find the object. The first person to find it is the winner.

▲ A girl playing Hopscotch in Nigeria. Hopscotch is believed to have originated in Africa, but it may have come from Asia. It is played with different rules in different parts of the world.

Spinning tops in ▶ Sierra Leone.

Play the game: Hyena Race

This game is played a great deal in Somalia. Spiral race games like this have been played in Africa since before 3000 B.C.

You will need:
2 playing pieces per player
one die
paper
a pencil

1. Draw a spiral shape on the paper, and fill the shape with evenly spaced squares. Draw a well at the center of the spiral, and a village at the open end.

2. One of each player's pieces represents a hyena, and the other piece represents a mother.

3. The mother counters move first. Take turns throwing the die and moving your piece the number of squares shown, starting from the village. Once your piece reaches the well, you need to throw a six to start the journey back to the village. The first person back is the winner.

4. The winner takes his or her hyena piece and starts the journey again. This time, the piece moves twice the number of squares shown on the die. If the hyena overtakes any mother pieces, the mother pieces must be taken off the board—they have been "eaten" by the hyena.

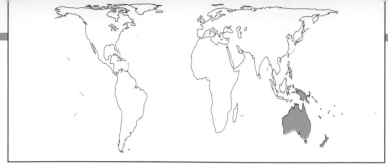

The Pacific

The Aboriginals of Australia have many traditional games that have been passed from generation to generation via songs and stories. Many of the games imitate adult life and can teach children various skills. In Central Australia, boys play a game in which they throw their spears at a disk made of bark that is rolled along the ground. Girls play a game where they use leaves as puppets. The leaves are laid out on the ground to tell the stories of the players' families and where they live. This game is called Muni-Muni.

A number of games are played only at certain times of the year, often because the materials used in the games change from season to season. In the fall in Australia, children drill a hole into a quandong nut and put a string through it. One player's nut is laid on the ground and the other players try to break it with their nuts. Whoever breaks the nut wins the game.

Men playing Cricket in the ▶ Trobriand Islands.

There are over 25,000 islands in the Pacific Ocean. In the central region, about eight hundred islands are inhabited.

A number of traditional games are found on these islands, many played with string. These include the Cat's Cradle, which is a game played with a long piece of string looped several times around the hands. These "cradles" can be made into the shapes of fish or waves and traditionally may have been used to illustrate stories. Cradles have been made all over the world and there are many similarities between the shapes made, such as the "fish spear" shapes of the Native American peoples, which are very like those of the peoples of Papua New Guinea.

In Rarotonga, children play a game called Pere Toka. This is similar to checkers and is played with ten white and ten black stones on a grid. Players can move their pieces only to where the lines cross on the board. A player can jump over an opponent's piece if it is next to one of his or her pieces and there is an empty point behind it. Once a piece reaches the opposite end of the board, it becomes a king.

Other traditional games in the Pacific include throwing long darts and a game similar to bowling played with wooden disks. Girls in Tonga play Hiko, in which they have to sing a song while juggling nuts, oranges, or balls in time to the song.

Games all over the world have their origins in the lives and histories of of the peoples who play them. Most games are very old or have developed from games which are very old. For centuries, people have made use of their leisure time by creating ways to play with and challenge each other. Their use of

▲ In the Pacific region, games often focus on the sea. These lifeguards are taking part in a race as part of an annual life-saving carnival in Australia.

A girl juggling ▶ during a game of Hiko, in Tonga. The players must sing and juggle at the same time.

local materials like the quandong nut or duck-feather shuttlecocks together with distinctive languages used to chant rhymes and commands help to create the uniqueness of games found in various regions of the world. Yet, through the tradition of games we can also see the many similiarities among cultures, since so many of the same games are played far and wide.

Play the game: Hipitoi

The Maori of New Zealand have many traditional hand games. Hipitoi is a simple game for two players. It is similar to Simon Says.

1. The person who starts is the hipitoi, or leader. Both players have to make the same hand movements at the same time.

2. If you make different movements, it is the second person's turn to be hipitoi.

3. If both players make the same movements at exactly the same time, the first person to shout out "hipitoi ra" wins a point and leads the movements the next time.

4. The person with the most points after an agreed number of games (5, for example) is the winner.

The hands are very ▶ important in traditional Maori games and dances, as they are for many peoples of the Pacific region. They are used to tell stories, to pass on myths and legends, to describe people and places, and to communicate ideas and feelings.

Glossary

Bamboo A giant tropical grass.

Descendants The offspring—children, grandchildren, etc.—of a family.

Dice Cubes of wood or plastic with a number of dots (1 to 6) on each side. They are used in games of chance. A die is a single cube.

Checkers A game for two players, using twenty-four pieces on a square checkerboard.

Counters The game pieces used to represent players on a game board. They can be anything from small stones to molded plastic or metal pieces.

Cricket A game similar to baseball in that two teams play with a ball and bat. Each team defends its "wicket" and scores runs. The team with the highest score wins.

Graphics The use of diagrams, drawings or designs.

Guava A South American tree that grows a delicious fruit with a yellow skin and pink flesh.

Harvest The time of the year when ripened crops are gathered.

Hindu To do with the Indian religion of Hinduism.

Hyena A wolf-like animal with a howl like human laughter.

Inning A side or team's turn to play.

Jute A thread used for making sacks.

Kampong The name for a Singaporean or Malaysian village.

Leopard A large cat with a black-spotted coat, found in Africa and Southern Asia.

Lime A green citrus fruit with a very sharp taste.

Muslim Relating to the religion of Islam, a set of beliefs centered around the prophet Muhammad.

Pewter A mixture of tin and lead used for making drinking mugs and plates.

Parlor Traditionally, a formal room where guests are entertained. A parlor was often the setting for evenings of card games and other indoor games.

Quandong nut A small nut from the quandong tree of Australia.

Runs Points scored in baseball, cricket, or similar ball sports.

Settlers People who leave their own country to live in another place.

Shuttlecock A small, round piece of cork with feathers stuck in the end, used in a number of games around the world, such as badminton.

Simulation A type of game or activity where the players take on the role of a character engaged in a situation that mimics real or fantasy life. Simulation games are very popular video and computer games.

Sprite An elf or fairy.

Vineyard A place where grapes are grown and made into wine.

Word of mouth When an idea or story, is passed from person to person by speech rather than in writing.

Books to Read

Barrett, Norman. *Sport: Players, Games and Spectacle.* Timelines. New York: Franklin Watts, 1993.

Hicks, Peter. *Sports and Entertainment.* Legacies. New York: Thomson Learning, 1995.

Oakley, Ruth. *Board and Card Games.* Games Children Play. North Bellmore, NY: Marshall Cavendish, 1990.

Oakley, Ruth. *Games with Sticks, Stones and Shells.* Games Children Play. North Bellmore, NY: Marshall Cavendish, 1989.

Whitney, Alex. *Sports and Games the Indians Gave Us.* New York: David McKay & Co., 1977.

Information about individual cultures may also be found in the 48-volume Cultures of the World series by Marshall Cavendish Corporation (North Bellmore, NY), or in your library's encyclopedia.

Index

The games in this book come from many different peoples, have many different meanings, and are played in all sorts of ways. If you want to see when and why games are played, look at entries such as "festivals" and "religion." You can use the "peoples" entry to look up games from each of the different cultures mentioned in this book.